My Bedtime Prayer

Written by Tony McCaffrey, S.J.
Illustrated by Ginna Magee

 Loyola Press

This book is dedicated to the children of St. Ignatius Parish in Chicago.

Loyola Press
3441 North Ashland Avenue
Chicago, Illinois 60657

Library of Congress Cataloging-in-Publication Data
McCaffrey, Tony
My Bedtime Prayer/written by Tony McCaffrey; illustrated by Ginna Magee.
        p.   cm.
    Summary: A bear says goodnight to God, thinking of all the good that God has given him—
the moon and stars, loving parents, toys and a blanket, a guardian angel, and more.
    ISBN 0-8294-0966-1 (alk. paper)
    [1. Bears—Fiction. 2. Christian life—Fiction. 3. Bedtime—Fiction. 4. Stories in rhyme.] I. Magee,
Ginna, ill. II. Title.
PZ8.3.M1245Go 1997
[E]—dc21
                                                                                                                        97-16411
                                                                                                                        CIP
                                                                                                                        AC

      00 01 / 10 9 8 7 6 5 4 3 2

Goodnight stars,
in the heavens so bright

You twinkle and shine
and wink goodnight.

Goodnight moon,

God's night-light from on high

You take turns with the sun
brightening up the sky.

Goodnight tree,
with your branches so fine
Each waving goodnight
as I whisper mine

Goodnight wind,
as you whisper so gently

You join the Holy Spirit
to love and accept me.

Goodnight all my toys, you help me to play
You help me to learn and have fun every day.

Goodnight Mom and Dad,
I feel your love more and more
It fills up my room
and overflows out the door.

Goodnight children everywhere,
you all sleep well, too
Sweet dreams of the playground,
the beach and the zoo.

Goodnight Little Rabbit,
I care for you so
For in loving others,
I learn how to grow.

Goodnight blanket,
you keep me safe and secure
Like an angel's soft wing,
so lovely and pure.

Goodnight pillow, where my head gently lands
You're as soft as the palms of God's caring hands.

Goodnight guardian angel, my own special friend
You watch me each day and all night without end.

Goodnight Jesus,
my Savior so dear
With you at my side
I have nothing to fear.

Goodnight God,
you create all I see,
and you LOVE all you made
—especially me.

Goodnight God,
I love you and all that you made—

the stars,
Mom and Dad,
even pink lemonade.